My Evil Twin:

The Unspoken Word

My Evil Twin:

The Unspoken Word

FREDDIE "FREDDIE FINGERS" LEYBA

iUniverse, Inc.
New York Bloomington

My Evil Twin:
The Unspoken Word

iUniverse books may be ordered through booksellers or by contacting:

iUniverse
1663 Liberty Drive
Bloomington, IN 47403
www.iuniverse.com
1-800-Authors (1-800-288-4677)

ISBN: 978-1-4401-9899-1 (sc)
ISBN: 978-1-4401-9900-4 (ebook)

Printed in the United States of America

iUniverse rev. date: 6/10/2010

Artwork, written work, typed work, book layout, cover design, and editing, all done by
Freddie "Freddie Fingers" Leyba

Thank You!

My thank you!—

Thank you, mom, for making the "BIG" sacrificial moves you did in order for me to live. You also had to be my FATHER, sister, brother, and best friend at the same time, and not necessarily in that order either. I would have done, and will do the same for you. Last, but not least, I want to thank you for making everyone wonder how one WOMAN created a man's MAN! I just can't seem to thank you enough!

My Evil Twin's thank you!—

I would like to say a "special" THANK YOU to both sides of my family, ex-friends, ex-girlfriends, and the rest of the PENDING "Human Beings" who I've come across that ended up crossing me, you deserve more than a CROSS. Collectively, if it wasn't for your loyalty, security, positive aura, constructive criticism, and hoping for better, I wouldn't be who I am today, an "unsuccessful" MAN, ha... ha; wait, or is it the other way around, I don't know; all I know is that either way ya'll got me twisted!

Preface

The main object or ideal of this book of poetry is not only for you to beware, but to instill awareness. I want you to be aware of the motivations, situations, circumstances, and words of our everyday negative lives and how they all connect in a mysteriously, humorous way that can create something positive.

The reason why I call this book, <u>My Evil Twin: The Unspoken Word</u>, is because I was raised with respect, compassion, pride, dignity, and class, but the eras where I'm from have done anything and everything to make sure they contradict morals and values, which has created a dark, bitter, and witty half of me. I also call this book, <u>My Evil Twin,</u> because people often consider the truth as being evil.

Growing up, I was quiet, and sensitive to others' feelings, and when I did talk, I was never really heard or valued, which is how and why I came up with the subtitle, <u>The Unspoken Word.</u> My secondary meaning for the subtitle is just as simple as taking the opposite meaning of stand up poetry night, "The Spoken Word," just for the simple fact that my poetry is written, and was never told.

Contents

My Evil Twin:

The Unspoken Word

My Motivational Speech!

1-3-07

Money is not
The "root" of all evil,
But it's the people
That create these
Real life sequels.
When life knocks us
Down a level,
We often complain that
We aren't all equal.
After all the struggles
Of life's "hard labor,"
We still have to build up
Enough strength
To "dig" deeper.

Where Do We Go From Here?

1-3-07

After sex
After pleasure
After laughter
After pain
After going insane
After love
After hate
After change
After remaining the same
After thugs
After the consumption of drugs
After parties
After knowledge
After work
After all of the materialistic things
After the experience
After death!

U-turn

1-4-07

If I keep walking down this one-way street,
I'll be headed for Danger Lane
With Psychopath Avenue and Maniac Road
As the major cross streets.

Tic...Tic... BOOM!

1-5-07

1, 2, 3, 4, 5, 6, 7, 8, 9, 10, 11, & 12.
I used to think people
Were my worst enemy
Until I met myself.
I'm bad for my own health,
Much less for anyone else.
What am I thinking?
I can't have a relationship
When the only thing I have to offer
Is anger,
Which is the same reason why
My best friend
Became a stranger.
I'm headed for danger,
Or should I say,
You are.
I'm so crazy
That my own family
Disowned me.
What do you mean, blow me?
I'll blow you up.
Yes, I am an asshole and a bastard
Because I never knew my father;
However, he is well known
For his temper.
It's problems like these
And many more
That keep me loaded
And ready to explode.
I guess I'm just another
Walking "time bomb"
With a very "short fuse."

Keep Faith!

1-5-07

Most people think that
I'm living in "dreamland,"
But what those people don't
Understand
Is that I live on
A small land
Where I'm forced
To dream big.
My visions, ambitions,
And aspirations
Are enough to inspire
The whole nation.
For me to remain positive
In these times of demanding negativity
Is like negating Baby Jesus
From the nativity.
I can't let people's activity
Ruin what God has
In store for me,
Which can't be bought.

United State
of Mind

1-30-07

The world is at
A standstill.
How can we go anywhere
If we're standing still?
How do we have what it takes
To still be standing,
If we don't even stand
For what we believe in?

My Other Half!

2-5-07

Who are you?
Who am I?
How did we get here,
My dear?
Come closer
Because love knows no fear,
At least that's what I hear.
Although forever seems near,
I fear that we'll never
Make it there.
Before we were one,
We were identical twins
Separated at birth,
Somewhere on Earth,
Set out on a lifelong journey
With the persistence
To find the purpose
Of our existence.
I can't even speak,
Or write this
Without you finishing
My sentences.
Every time I see you
I'm blinded from reality.
A product of God,
In which I benefit
From your assets and profits.
I'm very content
With the way you were sent,
Especially in this beautiful package.
Our love is fragile,
Even though there are a few damages.
If we manage,
Me and you will make the perfect team
With all the advantage
For winning the game of life.
If we cross that line,
You'll make the greatest trophy
As my wife.

Lingering Love

2-5-07

I told you that
You're all I need
To get by,
And you waved goodbye
Just as fast
As you said hello.
Now, I'm a mellow
Type of fellow,
But I'm not slow,
I get it.
I supplied you
With water and nutrients,
So now you need
Time to grow,
Solo.
I guess I'm just stupid;
I don't blame you,
But Cupid,
For not pointing the arrow
In the right direction.
Now I'm stuck
Trying to figure out
Which hurts worse,
The thin line between
Love and hate,
Or that knife
I can't pull out
Of my back.
You forfeited the team,
Which means
I'm filling the open wound with
The love you lack.

Until Death Do Us Part!

2-13-07

We used to be allies,
And now we can't even see
Eye to eye.
We often fought our battles
Back to back,
But now that it's
Every man for himself,
We'll die
Side by side.

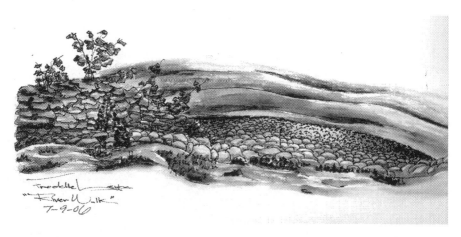

Senseless

5-5-07

What if I was blind
And couldn't read
Between the lines?
What if I was deaf,
But all you could hear
Was my every breath?
What if I couldn't smell;
Would the raw ingredients of life
Be that much harder to tell?
What if I lost the ability to feel;
Would life still have its appeal?
What if I couldn't taste;
Does that mean that
I should let everything
Go to waste?
What if I couldn't speak?
That is the very reason why
My pen leaks.

The Great
Depression 2

5-9-07

These days
It seems like I'm living in
A daze
Because life is
A maze,
An uncontrollable, overextensive,
Suffocated phase,
And I'm amazed.
People are doing things
As if they weren't raised.
The whole world is
Deranged
And in a rage;
This puts the people of
Great morals and values
In a tiny cage,
Afraid
Of the majority
Of bad news minorities.
I can't count on the priest to save me
Because I'm not young enough.
I also have to be careful about
Giving my female teachers an apple
Because that counts as an
Automatic "F,"
For fucking.
Our most reliable and necessary resource is
Trying to clean us out of life
Instead of trying to revitalize.

False Advertisement

5-19-07

Excess
Is not
Success!

Competition

5-20-07

Reality
Is no longer real;
If so,
Then tell me
How come
No one
Of this generation
Can feel.
We're all on the same path,
But I'm the one
That ends up becoming
Roadkill,
In a day and age
Where
The ongoing
Nightmare
Is for everyone
To have the same
Dream.

Survival of the Fittest

5-22-07

For you,
I will put my pride
Aside,
But never away,
It is far too much
To hide;
It seems this way
In order to abide
Nowadays.
My personality and upbringing
Are put
On the frontline
To defend
My capitalism,
Which means more to me
Than any war.
The only difference between this fight
And any other,
Is the fact that
No one has my back.
Every time I step
Onto the battlefield,
I feel like taking
Two steps back,
In hopes of falling down
The manhole
I call my shadow,
At least in that case
They will be able to walk
All over me.

Betrayal

5-23-07

The only way
You can get over me
Is to put me down,
Which seems to be
Your only recourse
Of remedy.
While I'm down there,
Could you step on
That crack
In my heart,
It won't hurt
Since you already
Stabbed me
In the back.

My Opening
Statement!

5-24-07

I would like to
Ask a question
Of the world.
Do you ever feel
Alone out there?
I know I do;
I feel alone
At this very moment
Speaking to you all.
I feel alone
Wherever I go
And whatever I do.
I'm alone, not because
I was born that way,
But because of who I am.
I figure if I derived
From your creator,
Then you wouldn't
Have a problem
With my character.
Since life isn't a movie,
Or a TV show,
There will be no
Sequel
Until we are all viewed as,
Thought of as,
And treated as equal.

Fami-lies

5-25-07

The world sees family
As a safe haven,
People you can count on,
People who share
The same culture,
And so on.
I say
If this place
Is no longer safe,
The number of people
You can count on
Has decreased,
And the only family tradition
That has been passed down
Is a history of emotional abuse, negativity,
And huge lack of success,
Then these allies
Have lied
To you.
All of a sudden the table
Has turned for the worst
During a Sunday family dinner,
The home cooked meals
Have become poisoned,
And the content of their conversations
And aura
Come off as if you are
An unwanted guest.
I guess that's why they say
The door is always
Open!

Now What!

6-7-07

I feel like I don't
Exist;
Dear God,
Is it wrong for me
To feel
Like this;
If it is,
Then it should
Also be wrong for your
So-called "children,"
To be senseless.
Are there any "human beings,"
Or has being human
Become just another fad.
I'm worried because
Our species
Has finally
Begun to fade-out.
Where does that leave me?

My Favorite Movie!

6-10-07

Time
Is no friend of mine,
But if it were,
At least I can
Count on it,
It has told more stories
Than these characters
Spreading fairytales
While living in fantasies.
The director
And producer
Often make wishes
Upon shooting "stars,"
Hoping that their hard work
Will pay on,
But only time will tell,
And it will take
Far longer than
A hour and a half.

Off Balanced

6-20-07

I never realized
How unfair
Life is
Until I had to
Pay fares.
I understand
My share,
But what about
Theirs.
You see,
I'm not selfish,
I'm just
Fair.

Give Me a Hand!

8-25-07

Someone,
Anyone,
And everyone,
Help me;
I've fallen
And can't get up.
I'm screaming
At the top
Of my lungs
From something that came
From the bottom
Of my heart.
I shouldn't have to yell
For you to understand
Another human being, as well.
I shouldn't have to spell
Words
You've already heard.
You should be able to
Just look at me
And read my
Body language,
Which speaks
Louder than I do,
But with a much
Stronger accent.
I just don't get it
Because I thought
"Love" was a
Universal language.

Rat Race

8-25-07

Many things run
Through my mind,
And if you look at
The human brain,
It looks like a maze;
That explains why people
Continue to go through their
Contagious cycles,
In hopes of getting out
To get the cheese,
By any means,
Which means
Ratting out
To get in.
Consequently,
We as "human beings,"
Expect to be rewarded
For our negativity,
Especially since
There's no telling
That once we cross the
Finish line,
There will be any type of
Award.

Me, Myself, and Irony

8-26-07

It's funny how people
Are everywhere,
But somehow
Not all the way
There.

Alienated!

9-4-07

There is a difference between
Being a sorry
"Human being,"
And being sorry;
These are the two types of people
That exist
On this planet;
There's no getting around it,
And no in between,
Damn it;
It's just as simply hard
As that.
It's obvious that
I'm not a part
Of this world.
The best
Usually stay far
Apart
From the rest,
Especially with a title
Like "Weirdo."
I guess I do
Deserve to be
On my own
Small planet after all,
Called
Pluto,
Which is not considered
A planet anymore,
Anyway.

The World's Motto

9-13-07

Go along
With whatever's
Going on,
No matter
If it's wrong.
Don't even bother
Trying to
Do something
Right.
Run along
And do you,
But make sure
It doesn't involve
Me.

Blankman

12-4-07

Do I exist,
Or am I here
Spiritually.
Whether spiritually good
Or bad,
People see me
As I see
Myself sometimes,
A nobody;
That explains why people
See right through me,
Walk into me,
Talk over me,
And can't hear me.

The Mirror
Reaction

12-4-07

Live is evil;
Love is evol;
These are a play
On words,
But no one
Is having fun
Here.

Play Offense!

12-5-07

We often set goals
For ourselves
So high
That it overcomes us
To the point where
The biggest obstacle in our lives
Is trying to climb over,
Or break down
That brick wall
We ended up building
On our way towards
Our goals.
For some of us,
That wall becomes
Too high
To see over,
And that is why
We eventually
Settle
To the bottom
Like heavy,
Bitter substance.

Bad Days

12-27-07

Another bad day
To add on
To the rest;
As often as they
Occur,
You would think that
They would give it a
Rest,
But instead,
The days will
Continue to increase
In multiple numbers
For the rest of my life.
Even though
My days are numbered,
I still can't count on
The day
That everything will be
Ok
Because that only happens
Once
In a "blue moon."

Suffocated!

12-27-07

At the first quarter
Of my life,
I feel like it's my
Last.
I'm beginning to
Decline versus
Progress,
And it's all due to
Stress
Put on by others
Who see me
As their mess;
It's all a part of
The plan to make
The best
Feel like he
Is less.

Happy New
Tears!

1-1-08

We made it
To another
Year,
In which
We celebrate
The hate
Of change
That puts us in
Fear,
And drowning in
Tears
Up to
Here,
Year after
Year.

Small World

1-8-08

It always seems
To be
The small people
Who make things out
To be
Bigger than they are.
I mean…
Ugh…
You know what I mean.
These people
Think big,
Talk big,
And live big,
But only in their eyes
Because in mine
"Lies" the truth.
They don't fail to
Realize
Their size
Because they "over-stood"
Their "downfall"
From the
Beginning of their
Demise.
You have to stand
Tall
And lookout
Because these people
Get in
Where they don't
Fit in,
Even though they're
Small.

The Wings of
My Dreams

1-8-08

I stay up
Late
On many
Nights
With all of these
Ideas
Flying around
In my head,
Trying to figure out
Which is
The best way
To get
The "worm"
While everyone's
Still asleep.

Overcoming
Obstacles

1-8-08

All of these
Blows
And innuendos
That people
Throw
At me
Leave me
Dizzy,
To the point where
I see
Stars;
Don't get it
Twisted though,
Those marks aren't
The stars.
The stars
Are symbolic
For my
Knowledge
And wisdom
That allows me to
Rise above them.

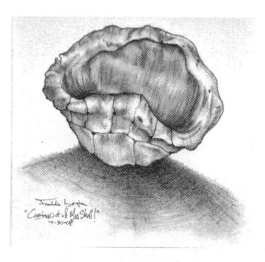

My Own Hero!

1-10-08

I'm like God
Of modern day.
I know it seems odd
For me to say,
But I can't control
My mastermind,
Or my well-mannered ways.
I'm nothing like
The average man.
So-called "men,"
Banned me from
Society,
So that makes me
An ex-man,
Mutated with superpowers
In order to defeat
Evildoers.

Get Me
Straight!

1-15-08

Sexuality,
Huummm…
What can I say?
What should I say?,
Or
What do I need to say?
I don't really need to say
Too much
Because everyone's obviously
Going to do
Whatever they want,
Literally.
When it comes to you,
Don't bother me;
Don't confuse me
With the rest of you.
I'm often looked at
By so-called
"Men,"
As feminine,
And
Women friends
Refer to me as a
"Gentleman;"
Either way,
I'm considered
As soft as they,
But I'm not
GAY!

Going Off!

1-18-08

They said to be afraid,
Be very afraid,
And they got me
That way,
Every second of my
Last days.
I'm so much afraid,
Just as much as
Women are afraid
To talk to me,
And
"Men" are afraid
To make friends
With me.
I'm afraid
Because there are
So many of them
And only one of me,
And none like me.
People plan to
Take me out
By an unmarked
Expiration date,
But I'm not their bitch.
I feel like
I'm in a lifelong,
Unscripted
Zombie movie
Where these
"People" are constantly
Trying to take a bite
To see what I'm like,
And in turn,
Turning me into
One of them.
I guess they're trying to end
My life the same way
Adam bit the apple
To begin this day.

Going Off!

(Still going!)

People can't stand to
See someone that
Stands outside
Of their TV set
Because I'm set
In the real
Reality show,
Better yet,
The movie,
But it's not
A blockbuster,
I just live on the
Same block
As these busters.

Mistaken for Weakness

1-24-08

When I talk
I scream;
When I walk
I kick.

Move On!

1-25-08

Leave the door
Open,
But don't spend
The whole day
Looking outside
The window.

My Shit List!

1-26-08

I'm the most easiest person
To get along with.
If you don't get along with me,
It's because you
Don't get along
With yourself.
Busters, marks, and cowards
Often can't stand me
Because they don't stand
Next to me,
So they stand
Away from me;
There is obviously
Some kind of
"Misunderstanding."
I tell them to
Take it for
What it's worth,
And they take me for
Granted,
But not anymore.

Private Caller

1-28-08

Hello.
Hello.
Hello.
You're calling me
From a private line,
And I'm calling you
Out of hiding.
You shouldn't be scared
To talk,
Especially since
I've known you for
So long.
You think I don't know
Who it is,
But you're the only one
That I don't know anymore.
Your only purpose
Is to hear
My voice
Through the only thing
That connects us
Together.
I'll admit,
"Caller,"
That you put
Our relationship on
"Hold"
For now,
I say that because
Every time I
"Flashback,"
I realize that I still
Love you,
Beside all of the things
You put me through.
I've done nothing to you,
But loved you, taught you things,
And helped you
In times of need.

Private Caller

(Line still in use!)

I gave you everything
I had
Including
A good man,
And you turned around
And ran
After you shrunk me
Down to your level,
Which made me go
Beside myself.
Knowing you,
You'll call me
For the rest of
Your life
And never say
A word.
In a confrontation,
The "wrongdoers"
Never admit they're
Wrong.
Since I happen to be
Bigger, mature, and
A "human being,"
I will hold,
And continue to
"Hold"
People accountable
For everything they do
Under the sun.
So the next time you call me,
You'll be calling your bluff.

Freddie Langton
"Private Caller"
7-20-08

My Turn!

2-4-08

Now that you've finally
Backed me into a corner,
I guess you still expect me
To back down.
Once again you've doubted
My size and my kind,
But like a true scorpion,
I won't hurt you,
I'll kill you
Softly
With one sting,
And walk around your body
Without even feeding off of
Your bullshit.
From now on,
I'll just
Maneuver around
"Cowards" manure.

Freddie Lyba
"Break Free!"
8-23-08

Daydreaming

2-4-08

They say
"Dreams come true;"
Well if that's true,
Then I'm never going to
Fall asleep again
Because every time I do
I die,
But somehow I continue to
Wake up from this nightmare,
Night after night.
Everyday I open my eyes,
I'm born again and ready to
Discover new things,
But just like a newborn,
I don't know anything, anyone,
And I don't know what to do.
In between the time
I awake and die,
I'm constantly trying to
Figure out
The purpose of this
Vicious cycle called
"My life,"
And I call that
"Daydreaming."

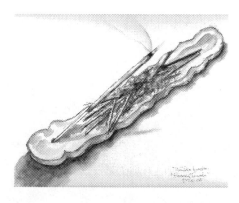

Life!

2-5-08

Accept change,
But don't
Expect a receipt!

Name Dropping

2-5-08

I see and hear
Your name
Wherever I go
And whatever I do.
Your name was hard
To be found,
That's only because
You were always around.
Now,
The only thing
I'm left with
Is that infamous sound.
At times I wonder
If it's you calling out
To me,
Or is it just you saying
Goodbye
For good.

Valentine's Day
Off

2-15-08

Yesterday was "lovers day,"
And since I'm not loved,
I spent the day working, watching,
And feeding lovers.
This was the first
Valentine's Day
That I spent alone
In a long time,
And I blame you,
Valentine,
Because you said
You would always
Be mine.

Between You and I

2-18-08

I'm so mad
I can scream right now.
Shit,
I'm screaming right now,
But you can't hear me.
My shrink told me one time
To go out into an empty field
And let it go,
And I did,
I lost my mind,
And began to decline
Ever since.
Now I see why people
Refer to them as shrinks.
I try to take everyone's advice,
But none of it seems wise.
I just don't know
What to do because
It seems like everyone is
Turning against me.
Even if I had health insurance,
There would still be no remedy.
I found out that
Fighting them mentally
Only destroys me mentally;
I can't fight,
Or kill them physically
Because I would only be carrying on
My family legacy.
They say the best thing to do is
Walk away,
But I still know what
They're going to say.
I respect myself
Too much to let them
Disrespect me,
But then again,
I respect myself too much to
Disrespect me.

For Rent!

2-19-08

Now that you're gone,
I find myself staring
Outside my window
Into your old house;
Sorry,
But you left the blinds open,
And no one is home.
The house very much symbolizes
Who you are to me now
As a person,
Just a nice big, beautiful, sweet,
And vacant structure
That has sheltered me
With good memories,
But is soon to be occupied by
Bad tenants.

Paying Doos

2-21-08

No matter who you are,
You have to "pay your dues"
In order to become
Someone.
Now, those dues vary
Depending on your situation,
But they all lead to shit,
And that's why I call it
"Playing in doo."
When the shit gets smelly, thick,
Or runny,
Always remember
That flowers grow with the
Support of manure.

Macks and Pimps

2-23-08

A Mack
Is a lady's
Man,
And a Pimp
Provides a man
With ladies.

Power in Numbers

3-3-08

Ever since my days
In elementary,
I saw the hierarchy
Amongst my peers.
I've watched them form
Groups, cliques, and gangs
At a young age
To hide their fears.
Of course,
Me being the odd one,
I was accepted into none,
But the Crips
Never let me drip
Blood.
Other than that,
My honesty
And goofy personality
Made me
Stand alone,
And also made those
Walks home
Very long.
I've been picked on
All my life,
But hardly picked
For any social
And physical activities
Because the guy who is
By himself
Is often seen as
The enemy,
Which in their eyes,
Develops a
"Lower-archy;"
To me,
This is not the case.
If there is power in numbers,
I'd rather be
Number one.

The Greatest
Reward

3-5-08

Competition
Is not
The mission
In our journey.
We should not be
Going against
Each other
For the same
"Bread and butter,"
Especially when
The "butter"
Spreads
No further
Than the love for
The next man.
I make sure
Whenever I take
A stand,
I take the next hand,
And head for the
Right direction
With nothing else
In common,
But the love
For one another.

Wis-dummies

4-17-08

Just because you're older,
It doesn't make you wiser.
In this age,
Age doesn't count
4
2
Much.
A person at 42 years of age
Acts like they are still
22 years old.
The fear of death
Can actually make you
Hold your breath.
These so-called "adults,"
Suffocate their growth,
And end up acting like
Their own,
Children that is.
It seems like every
Birthday,
People are literally
Reborn
At any given age,
And that explains why
They can't recall what
They did yesterday.
I think that everyone is
M.I.A.
On a vacation to
"Denial River,"
And floating downstream
Real fast.

Speak on It!

4-19-08

I'm going to
Set it off
Because you said
It's on,
And then I'm going to
Bring you
Back home,
Alone
After I touch bases,
Or maybe all lumped up
Together
Because busters
Always come in
Clusters.
I'm sick of you
Familiar faces.
They say if you can't beat'em,
Join'em,
But I say join them
Together.
Then beat the shit
Out of them
Because they're
Full of it.
They hate me because
I command respect,
Do it with finesse,
And don't follow the rest.
I must confess,
It's lonely at the top
With the best.

Love is Evol!

5-23-08

We as "human beings"
Often think of love
As a gift sent down
From up above,
But the doves
Are really crows,
And the bow
And arrows
Are from one of
"Hell's angels;"
No stupid,
Not Cupid,
That's how she
Got you.
She distracted you
With that red dress
And high-end designer shoes.
All you
Were thinking about,
Adam,
Was sticking your
"Worm"
In Madam's
"Apple."
Now you're
Burning,
Not from your genitals,
But in hell.

Evolution

5-25-08

From nomad
To no man!

The end

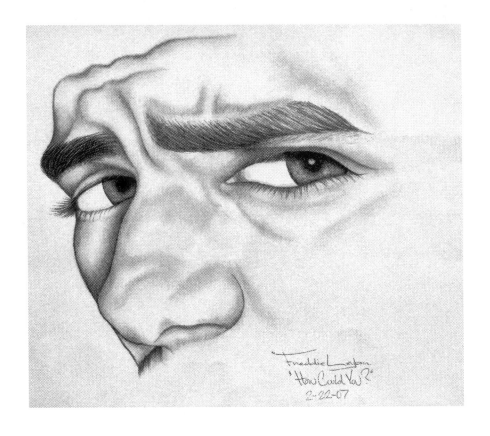

...for now!